My Darling John,

I Big present for you;
the whole of Sydney – well at
least the Black & white bits!!

With all my love

Anne
xxx

Sydney

in black and white

photography
ROBIN MORRISON

words
GLENN A. BAKER

Contents

A detail of Elizabeth Bay House.

Sydney

<p style="text-align: center;">~~~~~~~~~~</p>

The Best Address on Earth? The Emerald City? The Jewel of the Pacific? Sydney is accustomed to praise and makes no attempt to hide its splendours. A spacious, casual city of almost four million residents, it is absurdly blessed with natural beauty, from a deep, vast harbour once described as "shimmering like crushed diamonds in the midday sun" to a string of golden, full-bodied beaches stretching north and south from its rich cosmopolitan centre.

Over more than two hundred years, Sydney has evolved from a brutal, lonely penal colony to one of the world's truly great and enticing cities. Washed by the Pacific, warmed by a mild climate and enveloped by impossibly blue skies, Australia's harbour city is home to an array of humanity which adapts to its undemanding ways with ease.

Like the proud citizens of Venice, sybaritic Sydneysiders are at one with the ebb and flow of their watery environment, accepting almost endless sunshine as an entitlement rather than a privilege. The spirit of summer here is far more pervasive than the official season of a mere three months. Brash, open and largely uncomplicated, the people of Sydney have no doubts as to their place in the world … or their place in the sun.

<p style="text-align: center;">~~~~~~~~~~</p>

For those born here, it is all rather taken for granted. A Sydneysider in good standing myself, I spent the first ten years of my life just ten minutes walk from Coogee Beach, and, my, did I walk it. I raced billy-karts (with ball-bearing wheels cadged from a friendly local mechanic) down steep hills; I helped build and then stood in awe of towering Empire Night bonfires in a cliffside park; I clung for dear life to the rear of electric trams as they trundled through the tunnel on their way to Randwick and the City; and I claimed the beach as my own.

Almost every day, regardless of season, I let the blue Pacific pound me into the clean yellow sand. Tanned by the sun, made healthy by the fresh sea air, and turned cheeky by the touts, louts and drunks who inhabit any popular beach, I found that there was plentiful pocket money to be had by sifting through the compacted sand after the visitors had gone, or by cashing in discarded soft-drink bottles.

The soles of my feet were so resilient that I was impervious to the bubbling tar of Sydney footpaths in summer, and my hair was so full of salt and sand that it broke combs. I rose at dawn to ride around the darkened beachside suburbs with an obliging milkman and, whenever possible, came home from school by way of a mate's house sited tantalisingly near a sheer rock drop to the ocean. I trudged ahead of the afternoon breezes up the hill toward home as close to dark as I could get away with, a torn shirt hanging over my grubby shorts, dragging a piece of pine-tree wood behind me.

That Sydney has risen, in just two centuries and a bit, to be the bright, brash, glittering Xanadu at the bottom of the planet, is impressive. That it has done so by dint of determination and imagination, against a backdrop of unspeakable cruelty and isolation, retaining good humour and liberal tolerance along the way, is miraculous.

La Perouse on Botany Bay, Sydney's oldest aboriginal settlement.

The Dutch explorers who visited and mapped the west and north coasts of the island continent from early in the 17th century never made it around to the eastern side, except for Tasman's visit to Tasmania. When Captain James Cook sailed over from New Zealand in 1770 after observing the transit of Venus in Tahiti he did what the Dutch had considered inconvenient – charted the eastern coastline from the current NSW/Victorian border up to Cape York. Yet, although his *Endeavour* spent a week in Botany Bay, he did little more than poke his nose briefly between the heads of the harbour, name it Port Jackson after a Secretary of the Admiralty, declare it a safe anchorage, and depart.

The news Cook imparted to London of his discovery was hardly fevered, but English gaols were so overcrowded that prisoners were being held in rotting hulks on the Thames, and the recently independent America was disinclined to continue as Britain's dumping ground: there was plainly a use to which Cook's sheltered bay and its "fine meadow" could be put.

And so it was, at the hands of Home Secretary Lord Sydney (Thomas Townsend), who was responsible for the despatch, from Portsmouth on 13 May

1787, of eleven ships, a colony to found. Eight months and one week later, Captain General Arthur Phillip came to the rapid conclusion that Botany Bay had no water supply, and was flat and dreary. He sailed another ten miles north and ventured into Port Jackson, whereupon he declared it to be "one of the finest harbours in the world".

This was the place where 568 male convicts, 191 female convicts, 200 marines and 52 of their wives and children hoisted the colours and set up camp on the evening of Saturday 26 January 1788. Phillip considered calling it Albion, but named it Sydney, after the Home Secretary who had instructed the Admiralty to send this band of brave brigands and their gaolers halfway around the world.

The Sydney area was inhabited by Aboriginals of the Eora people; a part of the oldest surviving race on earth, whose origins extend back, it is said, beyond 70 000 years. These indigenous people did not so much use the land as harmoniously co-exist with it. They changed little except by fire, they built only simple dwellings, they left no physical mark beyond some cave paintings and rock carvings. This appeared then, in geographical terms, the blankest of canvases, the purest of clays. There was no written history, there were no dates to refer to from either Aboriginal or European. To the white settlers, it looked like a clean slate on which to draw a nation, and so they did, to the destruction of the Eora people.

Sydney *was* that new nation and, contentious though the assertion may be, remains so. It was, is, perhaps always will be the conduit through which Australia is sustained and through which it manages to make an impact in every area of endeavour. Melbourne has an entrenched establishment with political and financial clout; Brisbane is the "county seat" for the planters and herders of the most agriculturally viable state; and Perth is the power base for the country's inestimable mineral deposits. That gives all of them a vote at the boardroom table – but not the right to sit at its head.

Sydney has the pace, the vigour, the openness, the culture, the tingling licentiousness, the edge of menace, the greed, the wealth, and wears it all with a self-sufficient smirk plastered across its broad, freckled, suntanned face. It has Balmain boys who never cry and William Street girls who wouldn't know how. It has the national television networks, the publishing houses, the record companies, the flamboyant lawyers and the only flash millionaires who seem able to stay out of jail. And, most important of all, it has the bloody grandeur, mate.

As any Sydney cab driver will tell you, the Yarra is a muddy puddle masquerading as a river, the Torrens and Swan are not much better, and Moreton

Bay is a mere dent in the coastline. But Sydney Harbour, now there's a waterway! It is more stirring, more beautiful as a natural setting for a modern city than any San Franciscan or citizen of Rio would dare submit for consideration.

We Sydneysiders talk endlessly about our harbour – but we also use it, as a physical and spiritual gathering point during times of celebration and ritual. From floggings to fireworks, executions to extravaganzas, opera to oyster-eating, the harbour is a stately stage. Even when there is no pageantry – no 18-foot yachts hurtling through the heads in a mad dash toward Hobart, no *QEII* gliding toward its mooring at Circular Quay – the surface can be as busy as the ice rink of a European park. Red water taxis skim across the swells left by lumbering Manly ferries. Warships return to Garden Island Dockyard from some unspecified manoeuvres, while a lone windsurfer

A porker and poultry in untroubled residence at Pyrmont.

battles to stay upright and a news helicopter swoops down to film the multi-million-dollar mansion of a social butterfly.

Sydney has 60 kilometres of coastline on the seaward side, and 240 kilometres of harbour foreshore, every inch of it as valuable as Tokyo's Ginza. Since the first successful merchants of Sydney Cove sought to remove themselves from the squalor of the penal colony, the rich have known where to build their palaces, tennis courts and swimming pools, site their docks, and erect their no-trespassing signs. Close to the city, the heavily populated northern edges of the harbour can resemble the shores of the Bosphorus, while the commercial zones from Circular Quay around to Darling Harbour and Pyrmont are not unlike Manhattan, Hong Kong and Singapore. But along the opulent, lushly foliated inlets, bays, points and heads between the city and the ocean, with any land not claimed by parks, zoos and public beaches, comparisons are harder to pin down. This is where the myth of egalitarian Australia is effectively shredded.

～～～～～～

The ocean was really no big deal in Coogee – it was like growing up in the shadow of a mountain: you only miss it when you move away. I saw the harbour from the Manly Ferry and the Taronga Zoo Ferry, but was more interested in ice cream and orang-utans than a stretch of water that didn't even have a decent wave. In any case, I'd turned my attention inward.

Sydney also means suburban sprawl, to which I was introduced in the red-brick, red-tiled, two-bedroom Earlwood house of a frosty great aunt, and by a wily, Depression-hardened and surprisingly athletic grandmother, who was prepared to lead her first grandson around her old haunts. As she knew the city like a sweeper, and the suburbs almost as well, and as I was reading books at a rate beyond the parental purse, a natural partnership was formed. Using her war widow's rail pass and her capacity to scatter any human barriers with the swing of a handbag, we would make our way westward along the Bankstown line, alighting at Redfern, Burwood, Hurlstone Park, Canterbury, Campsie, Belmore, or any other station within walking distance of St. Vincent De Paul thrift shops or their equivalents. Then, laden with a new supply of Famous Five or William adventures and nourished with a Sargeants meat pie, I would return to my grandmother's rented semi-detached in Forest Lodge or Glebe and read myself to sleep, while she listened to radio plays and chortled loudly, with sublime disregard for all who failed to share her moments of pleasure.

Sydney's history is dotted with originals, eccentrics and oddballs, who are not so much tolerated as warmly embraced, and then greatly missed when they shuffle off to wherever expired iconoclasts go. There was Billy Blue, the black ferry captain of the Macquarie era, who might or might not have been a convict but was certainly a clown, a beggar and a septuagenarian groom. Blue's Point today perpetuates his memory. There was Francis de Groot, a furniture manufacturer who made an unscheduled one-horse cavalry charge during the opening ceremonies of the Sydney Harbour Bridge in 1932, and slashed the ribbon with his sword before Premier Jack Lang had the chance to do so officially. Declared sane, he was fined a fiver and sent on his way. Then there was Bea Miles, a woman of means and learning who read from Shakespeare in the streets, went shark fishing with a knife gripped between her teeth and refused, on principle, to pay bus or taxi fares.

A tile pattern to pull any felon up short, in Sydney's old Court House.

Hyde Park Barracks, designed for Governor Macquarie by Francis Greenway in 1819.

The city has been graced with a grand procession of what it likes to call "identities", men and women of sometimes dubious morality but undoubted charisma, from the worlds of inn keeping, horse racing, brothel-keeping, letters, entertainment, car sales, politics and the police force. No less entertaining are the audacious street people — the winos, derelicts, nutters and babbling pram pushers.

I have not seen him about for a few years now but I remain fascinated by an old man who frequented the Town Hall area clad in a large sandwich board inscribed with a rambling diatribe on the evils of psychiatry. I do still see an aged, severely stooped woman pushing all her possessions around Sydney in a long, sturdy steel trolley. And I would rather not see again a towering, bald, armless behemoth of a man, clad in a ballet tutu, who runs out in front of cars on Victoria Road at Drummoyne.

Much has been written about the convict origins of our much celebrated anti-authority attitude, but the people of Sydney are actually no less law-abiding than their peers in other Western cities. What they do possess is a healthy cynicism for the established order of things. Sydneysiders do not celebrate the success of their own, they are openly suspicious of it. Getting "too big for your boots", "sucking up" to the teacher or the boss, or rising higher than your mate is still virtually unforgivable behaviour.

On blood-drenched shores where rebellious wretches were administered 500 lashes, is it odd that a hardy species of wary, knowing, cunningly avaricious, pleasure-seeking, larrikin people should have evolved? There was courage and at the same time an intractable venality — the same elements which fleck the fabric of Sydney today.

Charles Darwin, who made his way to Sydney in 1836, was so greatly impressed by the policy of released convicts being granted land that he wrote, "As a means of making men outwardly honest — of converting vagabonds most useless in one hemisphere into active citizens of another, and thus giving birth to a new and splendid country, a grand centre of civilisation — it has succeeded to a degree perhaps unparalleled in history."

Well, a relatively distinct human being did come out of that experiment. Admittedly, he may be a blue-singletted, heavy-booted labourer tossing back schooners of beer in one of Sydney's public bars, or she may be a professional surfer pulling in more than the Prime Minister each year; but they stand out in a crowd. In fact, Sydney's crowds stand out. Only Tel Aviv and New York can seriously compete with Sydney for the honour of being the most cosmopolitan city on earth. There are more languages spoken in Sydney than in the United Nations dining room. This, in a country once known best to the outside world for its iniquitous White Australia Policy!

The rich ethnic diversity is conveniently attributed to the post-war migration boom, which began in 1947 with the arrival of the *General Heintazelman* and its human cargo, the wretched refuse of Europe's wars, pogroms and social disintegration, and continued with boatloads of assisted-passage settlers. But, in fact, it stretches back to the very beginnings of the colony: of the 83 000 convicts transported to New South Wales between 1788 and 1840, more than 3000 were non-British and more than 100 were British blacks. The Goldrushes, 70 after the First Fleet, brought in large numbers of Chinese, while the pearling boom in the Western Australian port of Broome just before World War I attracted Japanese, Filipino, Malay and Indonesian divers. Many of these found their way to Sydney.

The Strand Arcade in the city.

Between 1947 and 1971 came a greater boom: some 75 per cent of Sydney's population expansion was a consequence of migration, mainly from Britain, Holland, Germany, Malta, Greece, Italy, Yugoslavia, Turkey and Lebanon. These days the process continues with the arrival of new settlers from Vietnam, Cambodia, Hong Kong, the Philippines, Chile, Peru, South Africa, Tonga, Samoa, and New Zealand.

The injection of new dimensions into Sydney life chipped away at the old evils – parochialism, the colonial inferiority complex, xenophobia, a distrust of intelligence and sophistication, and adherence to all things British.

In the nineties, Sydney is cosmopolitan, and is thus one of the great cities of the world to eat in. One can consume Laotian, Egyptian, Syrian, Nigerian, Argentinian and Creole cooking all in the one suburb, and if a known cuisine is not served somewhere in Sydney, it is only a matter of time before an entrepreneur finds the right chef and lays the tables.

Things have also changed sexually. It is hard to believe that morality police were seizing Beardsley prints and raiding progressive book stores in the sixties, or that the nude tableaux in *Hair* at the end of that decade could only be performed in near blackout conditions. What was hidden from sight at the Metro Theatre in 1969, is now on vivid display every night on the main thoroughfare to the Cross, Sydney's equivalent of Times Square or the Reeperbahn. Kings Cross was once Queen's Cross but, more importantly, it was a bohemian village peopled by fairly harmless eccentrics and rascals, a place that possibly did have a heart of gold hidden beneath minor deviations essential to the textured life of any city. Now teenage prostitutes of both sexes ply their tawdry trade around Kings Cross and Darlinghurst; drugged under-age girls are found naked and dead in hotel rooms. Blind conservatism has been replaced by blind indifference.

Nearby Oxford Street, with its pubs and clubs, is the holdout of the gay community, which each year stages an outrageously camp Gay Mardi Gras, a giant tongue-poke at the straight community. Sydney is the world's second most homosexual city after San Francisco, with an estimated 15 per cent of the population leaning in that direction. This does not go down all that well with some brawny blue-collar workers, who may spend Saturday night in town "poofter baiting".

These differences underline the new reality that Sydney is not one city but many — geographically and socially. It sprawls over an area of 670 square miles and has over 750 listed suburbs and localities. To drive from the southern suburb of Cronulla to the northern suburb of Palm Beach would take over two hours; to return via the far western suburb of Emu Plains would require more than three. To millions of Sydneysiders, the city is a place they see on television when Bicentennial fireworks or the Sydney to Hobart Yacht Race takes place. With ready access to large suburban shopping centres, to sporting venues such as Eastern Creek Raceway, the State Sports Centre at Homebush and the Parramatta Football Stadium, and to recreation centres like the Australia's Wonderland theme park, many recognise no pressing need to add to the congestion of the Central Business District.

Then again, many do: on Friday and Saturday nights it is shoulder-to-shoulder down at The Rocks, the gentrified site of early Sydney settlement across Circular Quay from the Opera House and Bennelong Point. At all other times, tourists swarm over this artfully preserved wedge of Sydney history, drinking in the "quaint" pubs, admiring in the craft and visitors' centres, and buying souvenirs in the boutiques.

Around Dawes Point at Darling Harbour, it is more a case of reclamation than restoration. For a hundred years, Darling Harbour was an anchorage in decline, a factory zone, a rail goods yard, an industrial eyesore and a grimy urban slum. Then came grandiose schemes for a harbour promenade and complex of public facilities, which was all supposed to be in place by the 1988 Bicentenary. Of course it was not but it would be churlish to dwell on that in the light of what has materialised, and how Sydney has taken it to heart.

Thousands without number now put the kids in the family sedan and make their way eagerly to Darling Harbour, where they can divest themselves of disposable income at the 200 shops of the Harbourside Festival Marketplace, edify themselves at the Maritime Museum and Sydney Aquarium, amuse themselves on the Monorail, be entertained at the Tumbalong Park mini-amphitheatre, spiritually unwind in the Chinese Garden and maybe drink at the Pump House brewery. During the week they may well return to attend a function at the Exhibition Centre or the 3500 capacity Convention Centre.

Mateship, contemplation and cold beer at a Glebe pub.

The acceptance of Darling Harbour tells us something about Sydney's outgoing spirit. It may be the weather, it may be the location, it may be the standard of living or it may just be a sense of an inalienable right to be go and enjoy at will: whatever the motivation, there is no shortage of attendance. A mid-week night game at the Sydney Cricket Ground can draw over 30 000. Multiple cinema complexes are as busy as Tokyo subway stations. An annual City To Surf Marathon is contested by up to 37 000 amateur and professional runners. Racetrack bookies rarely cry poor.

Sydney loves to be entertained, by day and by night. International concert

Street theatre at the Saturday markets in Paddington.

acts sweep through town each year, taking the big money out of willing pockets. The change that is left goes to the domestic fare. On almost every night in Sydney it is possible to witness performances by well over 100 worthwhile acts, in the areas of rock, jazz, folk/country, blues, cabaret, harsh street comedy and the undefinable. In all but the major concert events, considerable alcohol consumption goes with live entertainment. A rowdy good time comes well ahead of meaningful metaphysical experience. Almost every workingmen's club reverberates to youth-oriented acts, and most sizable suburbs boast vast concrete beer barns jammed with between one and two thousand boisterous patrons. "We have the best club and pub scene in the world," hard-rocking mega-star Jimmy Barnes once said. "You go to New York and you can't see as many bands playing as you can in Sydney. Los Angeles closes at 1 a.m. and London's only got about five good venues. Good bands here can go out and work any day of the week. That's why they're so intense and unique." No less intense, it can be argued, than the city's orchestras, opera troupes, dance companies, comedians, choral societies, chamber music groups, folk ensembles, jazz big bands, and bush bands. Although mass Australia has, traditionally, reached for its shotgun at the mention of the word "culture", operatic and symphonic concerts are moving beyond hallowed halls. Each January, as part of the extensive Festival of Sydney, The Domain, a large expanse of parkland behind Parliament House, plays host to both a free symphony concert and free opera performance. Past years have seen Dame Joan Sutherland, Dame Kiri Te Kanawa and Joan Carden take the open air stage before audiences of 40 000.

I haven't been back to Coogee for years and I don't need to scour junk shops for books any more. Sydney means different things to me now. I live in a spacious and sedate middle-class suburb and raise children to be as tolerant and good natured as I believe Sydney expects of them.

After 40 years I know her intimately, yet I never cease to discover new reasons to be both impressed and depressed. Like all Sydneysiders I have begun to complain about smog, traffic and the traffic police; I see prices getting higher; and there are places I would rather not walk after dark.

On the other hand, cultural diversity means that in Cabramatta, with its large Vietnamese population, I can buy Saturday lunch at a busy smorgasbord eatery, with plates of peppered pigs feet flying past my left ear as I try to negotiate for humbler fare. Then there is the bold imaginative Power House Museum at Ultimo where due homage is paid to technology, science and the applied arts. And the haphazard markets in Balmain, and Paddington where it is still possible to smell patchouli oil and pick up a real cheap poster of Che Guevara.

Make no mistake, Sydney can be as irritating as it is entrancing, as obstinate as it is accomodating, as ugly as it is beautiful. But when it is beautiful it shines.

GLENN A. BAKER
June 1992

The Waterfront

*The city skyline from Farm Cove –
hints of classic Manhattan
and Fritz Lang's Metropolis.*

*Overleaf: So many views, so
many perspectives. The city from
Watsons Bay.*

A naval warehouse at the Royal Edward Victualling Yard in Pyrmont, with outside fire escapes of a style now rarely seen on Sydney buildings.

Opposite: Morning homework on the Lavender Bay Ferry, swiftly slicing across Port Jackson, under the Harbour Bridge to Circular Quay.

~~~~~~~~~~

Above: Port Jackson from Cremorne Point.

~~~~~~~~~~

Below: Once underway, the Mosman Bay Ferry will emerge into Port Jackson between Curraghbeena Point and Robertson's Point, then dodge the stop-for-nothing Manly Ferries as it crosses the harbour and rounds Bennelong Point to join the aquatic scramble at Circular Quay.

Opposite: From the Park Hyatt Hotel on Dawes Point across Sydney Cove to the Sydney Opera House on Bennelong Point – one of the finer harbour views.

Sydney Opera house from the Harbour Bridge. Danish architect Joern Utzon's structure is an emblem of Sydney as internationally familiar as the Egyptian Pyramids.

Cocktail hour on Sydney
Harbour; the ambience is as
intoxicating as the alcohol.

Neutral Bay, a middle-money
harbour suburb, where
merchantmen from foreign ports
once dropprd anchor and declared
themselves friend or foe.

To some, warships in Sydney Harbour are a comforting presence.
The harbour itself has known direct naval warfare only once: when a Japanese
midget submarine sank a ferry and killed nineteen naval
ratings on 31 May 1942.

Busy doing nothing on a Pittwater wharf.

Opposite: A jogger making his way along Mrs Macquarie's Road at Mrs Macquarie's Point toward Mrs Macquarie's Chair. Although she spent only twelve years in Australia, Elizabeth Macquarie, wife of well-regarded NSW Governor Lachlan Macquarie, has the distinction of being commemorated in a greater variety of place names than any other person in Australian history. Even her maiden name, Campbell, was put into active service in the young colony.

Similar exertion at Darling Harbour.

If you have it, flaunt it!

Sydney Harbour Bridge, illuminated for harbour adornment and night-time use.

*Undisturbed fishing
at Church Point on Pittwater.*

35

Cliffside house at North Bondi.

The Macquarie Light, built on South Head
in 1853 near the site of the original 1817
Macquarie Lighthouse, Australia's first. There
have been structures on this critical point since
a wood-fired ironbasket light was installed
in 1790.

~~~~~~~~

The Gap, on the seaward side of South Head.
~~~~~~~~

A Harbour foreshore freely available to all.
Fishing at Woolloomooloo Bay, jogging along the edge of The Domain.

Japanese tourists survey Sydney Harbour from the Opera House on Bennelong Point.

*A prime picnicker's view from Shark Bay
at Nielsen Park.*

~~~~~~~~~~

*Opposite: There are constant reminders in
Sydney of the city's colonial past, when it was linked
to the mother country by the sturdiness of sail and
the grace of God.*

~~~~~~~~~~

North Sydney Olympic Pool on the edge of the harbour.

*Sydney Harbour Bridge from Observatory Park on
Millers Point.*

Architecture

Houses in Paddington, one of the early residential suburbs which took shape in the decade following the 1832 offer of assisted passage to free settlers from the old country.

Opposite: From Millers Point, the omnipresent Sydney Harbour Bridge.

*Sydney Harbour Bridge
from road level.*

The distinctive external facade of the Convention Centre at Darling Harbour.

Many periods and styles together in Pitt Street,
near the Town Hall.

Opposite: Sydney's omnipresent British heritage, emphasised by the Queen Victoria Building and splendid Sydney Town Hall, and constrasted by the modern Coopers-Lybrand Building, designed by the firm of Rice Daubney.

C&L

The superbly refurbished
Queen Victoria Building.
A tribute to the time of royal
glory, still in place in these days
of fledgling republicanism.

A stairwell in the Queen Victoria Building, designed by City Architect George McRae as Sydney's fruit and vegetable market and built in 1898. Occupying an entire city block, the 200-metre-long structure fell into serious disrepair before being superbly restored at a cost of $75 million. It reopened in November 1986, and houses 200 elegant Victorian-fronted shops.

Victoria Barracks in Oxford St,
Paddington, built in 1841,
designed by Colonial Engineer George
Barney, who was also responsible for
what we now know as Circular
Quay and for turning Pinchgut
into Fort Denison.

*Victorian architectural details
preserved on a Hunters Hill Building*

The origins of Australia's banking system, lovingly preserved in Sydney's Rocks area.

The Lord Nelson Brewery Hotel, on the corner of Kent and Argyle Streets in The Rocks, has survived as a legendary waterhole since 1841. It was built as a three-storey Georgian private house in whitish sandstone in 1834, for ex-convict William Wells.

Left: A Federation house, Balmoral. The highly romantic style of Federation architecture, known originally as Queen Anne, proliferated from the 1890s to around 1910.

Terrace houses in Potts Point, the first residential area to be settled after Sydney Cove.

Paddington terrace houses – aesthetically delightful but physically suffocating – with elaborate decorative ironwork known as Sydney lace (some twenty patterns of which are still to be found).

The imposing Sydney Tower in the background and a
sculpture outside the Art Gallery of New South Wales.

~~~~~~~~

On the corner of York and Market Streets, Sydney's
sleek monorail, which polarised the city's opinions and
emotions as no construction before it. Fire remains in the
bellies of both camps and the future of this particular
rapid transport system is far from guaranteed.
~~~~~~~~

Skygarden in Castlereagh Street.

The Strand Arcade, reminiscent of Dickensian London and emblematic of
imperial splendour, links George Street with the Pitt Street Mall. Gutted by fire
in 1976, it was faithfully restored in Classical Revival style.

The magnificent State Theatre,
Sydney's most ornate small theatre.
It was designed in New York by
Henry E. White and John Eberson
as a 1920s cinema palace, and its
Grand Assembly Room was
inspired by Louis XIV's salons at
the Palace of Versailles. The grand
Wurlitzer organ which rose from the
bowels of the building to delight
movie patrons during the Depression
is still in use, though only for
special occasions.

Above: One of the State Theatre's many marble statues in its ornate alcove.

Left: The foyer of the State Theatre in Market Street, opened in 1929 and beloved for its crimson velvet drapes, gold-leaf doors and Czechoslovakian crystal chandelier. Today, it plays host to rock concerts and the Sydney Film Festival.

Hothouse pyramid in the Botanical Gardens off the Domain.

Canyons of glass and steel at the harbour end of the Central Business District.

The Quayside Tower at Circular Quay - which is actually square, just as Australia Square is round. This perversity is no doubt related to the way water runs down Australian plugholes - clockwise.

Reflected outline of city skyscraper.

Sydney Harbour Bridge - The Coathanger. Its opening in 1932 halved an annual cross-harbour ferry passenger flow of fifty million and effectively opened up the city's northern regions. Though hardly more than adolescent, it is now one of Sydney's dearest and most beloved friends. Eminently functional, totally reliable.

Sydney Tower, atop the Centrepoint shopping arcades, the tallest structure in Australia, at 1000 feet (304.8 metres), Known affectionately as The Plunger.

The "sails" of Sydney Opera House, a still-startling piece of design and construction which elicits extraordinary descriptions. Blanche d'Alpuget, has likened it to "an albino tropical plant root bound from too small a pot" Robert Hughes thought it "a magnificent doodle".

Leisure Spaces

Table chess at a Pacific pace in Nielsen Park.

Overleaf: Sunday lunch at Cottage Point Inn on Cowan Creek in Ku-ring-gai Chase National Park. Seafood under umbrellas amid untrammelled bushland no more than forty minutes from the city's heart.

A shark-netted beach and the alluring city
seen from Nielsen Park.

New South Wales Governor Lord Carrington marked Australia's
first centenary on 26 January 1988 by dedicating the 216-hectare
Centennial Park for the use of the people of Sydney. It is a serene area
comprising lawns, trees, ponds, ducks and palms, disturbed only by the
murmur of hidden lovers, the swish of pared - down bicycles and the
sighs of Tai Chi practitioners.

Closed from sunset to sunrise, Centennial Park throws open its gates
in the misty early morning to the Police Riding School and the fanatically fit.

Warming to the working
day with an early morning cycle
in Centennial Park.

80

The Bulletin *founder Jules Francois Archibald, a satirist of considerable charm, is most commonly associated with the fiercely contested annual art prize which bears his name. His other great contribution to the city he adopted in 1878 was the Archibald Memorial in Hyde Park - a bronze statue commemorating the unity of purpose of France and Australia during World War I.*

~~~~~~~

Originally modelled on Kew Gardens rather than its London namesake, the green rectangle of Hyde Park houses the Anzac Memorial and provides a compact perimeter around which have been draped a cathedral, church barracks, synagogue and museum. In its wooded heart, squirrels thrive, eccentrics rant, workers nap ...
~~~~~~~

... and mates check each other.

Above: Boisterously flying the flag for the Old Dart at Sydney Cricket Ground, during an Australia vs. England test match.

Sanctified soil: Sydney Cricket Ground, where Donald Bradman made 452 not out in 1929. Like The Hill - a littered mound where zealots engaged in ritual confrontation - the spirit of the dignified, gentlemanly Bradman is now part of history.

Surfers walk through silent Bronte Cemetery, where the inhabitants have one of the best views in Sydney.

Opposite: Sailing on Pittwater, near the Northern Beaches, with chilled Australian white wine doubtlessly in plentiful supply. "And to think we sent you bastards down here for punishment!" an Englishman once said to Australian actor Jack Thompson.

Confronting art in the Art Gallery
of New South Wales where the New
Eclecticism rules.

PLEASE
DO NOT
TOUCH

Verified by this resident of the
magnificent Taronga Park Zoo on
the harbour foreshores: Sydney -
the best address on earth.

Cafe culture was not part
of life for British colonists.
Unselfconscious outdoor dining
came with the post-war migrant
boom and the injection of
European flair.

People

The pubs of Darlinghurst, Kings Cross, Glebe and Balmain serve much the same
social functions as those of Dublin - conversation, lubrication, seduction and musical appreciation.

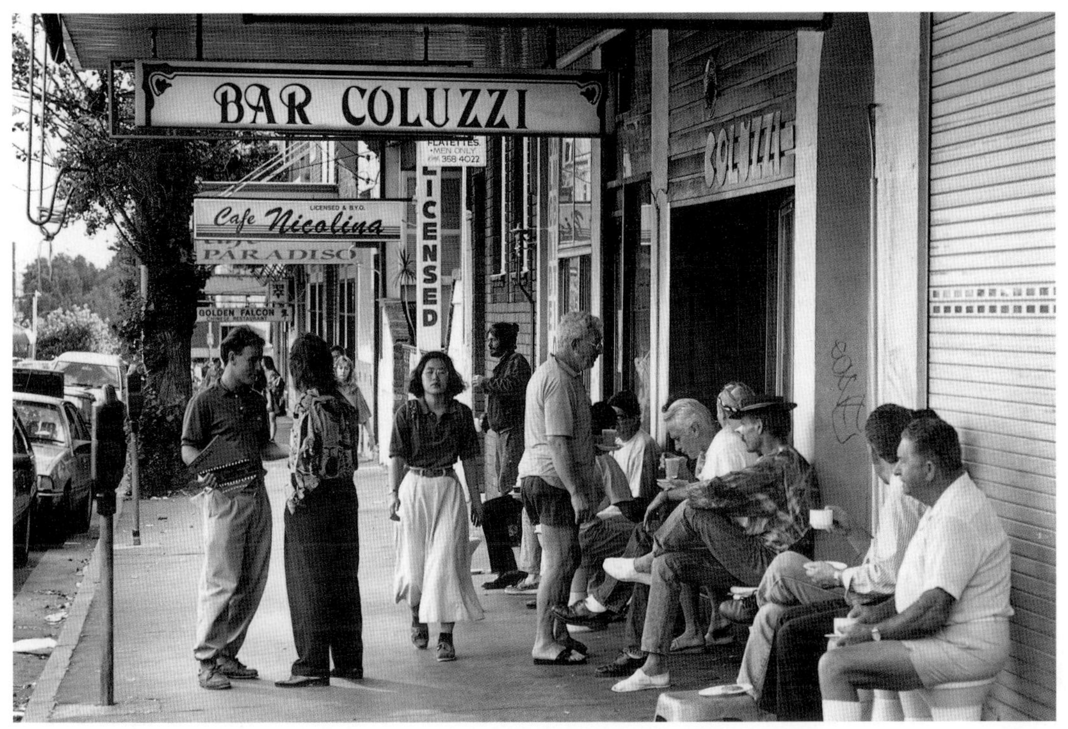

Coffee shops in cosmopolitan Darlinghurst - a less lascivious area than Kings Cross but no less intense.

Camaraderie or privacy on the worn wooden benches of a Glebe Point Road cafe.

The unbridled passions stirred by test cricket in the nineties.

Opposite: The Paddington concept of a nuclear family. Where else but Sydney would you find a border collie at home in a sports car?

Intricate cake decorating in the bohemian inner suburb of Glebe.

Contemplating the Headlands exhibit of New
Zealand art at the Museum of Contemporary Art on Circular Quay.

Outdoor birthday party in Nielsen Park.

~~~~~~~~

Basil Privett in greater suburban Canterbury, the red-roofed epicentre of Sydney's old western suburbs, where ducks still fly in formation on neat loungeroom walls.

~~~~~~~~

Lotteries!
Your best bet yet. 6-3
Official Agent
FREE!
GIANT POSTER
JACKPO
THIS THURSD
$2½ Milli
SCRATCH
FOR CASH
BINGO
Sunday
Telegraph
Govt plan
STAGGER
WORKING
HOURS
Harper
Collins

Community relations, Kings Cross style. A certain tolerance for the tawdry is necessary in a precinct where porn palaces adjoin chapels and late-night flesh factories become early-morning flower stalls.

Bagging an octopus at the Sydney Fish Markets on the Blackwattle Bay side of Pyrmont.

Sydney's voracious appetite for its own seafood is satisfied largely in the frantic Fish Markets at Pyrmont, where Greek stalls run by innumerable young Asians daily sell tonnes of fresh sea bounty. Red prawns are a staple.

Chinatown herbalist with a
parcel of intriguing ingredients.

YAMAHA

An appreciative if not terribly generous audience for a
Circular Quay busker.

Customised wet-weather gear in the beachside suburb of Balmoral.

Sleaze with ease:
preparing for the annual Gay
Mardi Gras, a cascade of
carnality which outrages as
many as it amuses.

NOT SINCE YOU SQUEEZED IT Y

Morning tea on impulse, between shops and home, in a Glebe bus shelter.

Chrome domes at the
Town Hall Square waterfall.

The languid pace of lawn bowls, the most
sedate, genteel and conservative of all Australian
outdoor sports.

1980's
SPORT
Australia - a nation of
sports men and women
who continue to achieve
on the world stage.

*A little flutter on the horsies,
Canterbury Races.*

116

Bookies at Canterbury Races - a hardy species eulogised by poets and chroniclers since convict strappers first lined up South African steeds at Hyde Park's northwest corner in 1810.

A middy and a yarn at the Glenmore Hotel in The Rocks.

The Beach

Overleaf: Sombre picnicking and surfing-for-the-practice at Palm Beach, the film-colony strip of pine-protected sand at the tip of Sydney's snaking northern peninsula.

~~~~~~~~~~

Reading on the sand at Manly's harbour beach near the ferry terminal.
~~~~~~~~~~

A languid laconic lifestyle at rocky Maroubra.

*The judging of the surf lifesaving championships at Narabeen Beach,
conducted with a diligence and an attention to detail that would not be
out of place at Centre Court, Wimbledon.*

*Opposite: Mother instructing
child in watery ways on Bondi Beach.*

The surf lifesaving Iron Men doing battle at Narabeen Beach. For the better part of this century, beachside families have sent their sons into unpaid service on behalf of the nautically inept with the same pride and sense of fulfilled duty that the Irish seem to feel on sending their male offspring into the priesthood.

*Left: The last vestiges of Bronzed Aussie
youth on Manly Beach participating in one
of the few social rituals Australia has
seriously sustained – surf lifesaving.*

*An arcane Bondi lifesaving rite
no doubt linked to tides and phases of the moon.*

Bronte Surf Club gave birth to Sydney's stomp music boom of the
early sixties. Creative footwork is still to be found down by the beach.

A self-absorbed juggler on Bondi Beach; not likely to be able to sustain himself on public alms.

〜〜〜〜〜

A late summer evening beach dance at Bondi, a district that has proven magnetic for immigrants from the Pacific, particularly disenchanted New Zealanders.

〜〜〜〜〜

Opposite: Happy snaps on a sodden though still seductive Bondi Beach. Those who shoot tourism and immigration posters set up their tripods on other days.

A dedicated lone surfer at Bronte.

Rock fisherman at Bronte.

Long-line surf fishing near Tamarama Beach, a precarious
pastime which regularly claims the lives of inattentive anglers.

Shift change at Bondi Beach.
One sunburned sybarite's day ends
as the evening promenade begins.

Annual Clean-up Day labourers at La Perouse Beach.

The rocks that have fallen in the past from Sydney cliffs provide picturesque contours on the sand below.

A quiet bay near Church Point, Pittwater.

Opposite: Bondi Beach, spoken of internationally in the same breath as Ipanema, Malibu, Waikiki, Kuta and St Tropez.

Bondi boogey-board boy.

The constantly sea-sprayed rock pool
at Bronte Beach.

~~~~~~~~~

Bronte Beach, south of Bondi,
where the first branch of the Life Saving Society
came together in 1894. The Surf King, the first
boat designed for the Australian surf, was
launched here in 1906.
~~~~~~~~~

Stately Balmoral Beach, with its fine white pavilion, ornamental bridge, and gardens, was declared a sacred and significant site by the Theosophical Society after World War I. Adherents to that particular faith are a little scarce on the ground in Balmoral these days and their holy amphitheatre has gone the way of their promised World Teacher.

The bedrock view of Tamarama Beach.

A Kevin Weldon Production

Published by Weldon Publishing
a division of Kevin Weldon & Associates Pty Limited
Level 5, 70 George Street Sydney NSW 2000 Australia

First published 1992

Designed by Catherine Martin
Printed by Griffin Press Ltd, Adelaide

National Library Cataloguing-in-Publication data

Morrison, Robin, 1944–
Sydney in black and white

ISBN 1 86302 231 7.

1. Sydney (N.S.W.) – Pictorial works. I. Title. (Series: Cities of the World
(Sydney, N.S.W.).

994.410630222

Cover photographs: North Sydney Pool and Sydney Harbour Bridge.
Opposite the title page: celebrations of the sixtieth birthday of the Harbour Bridge.

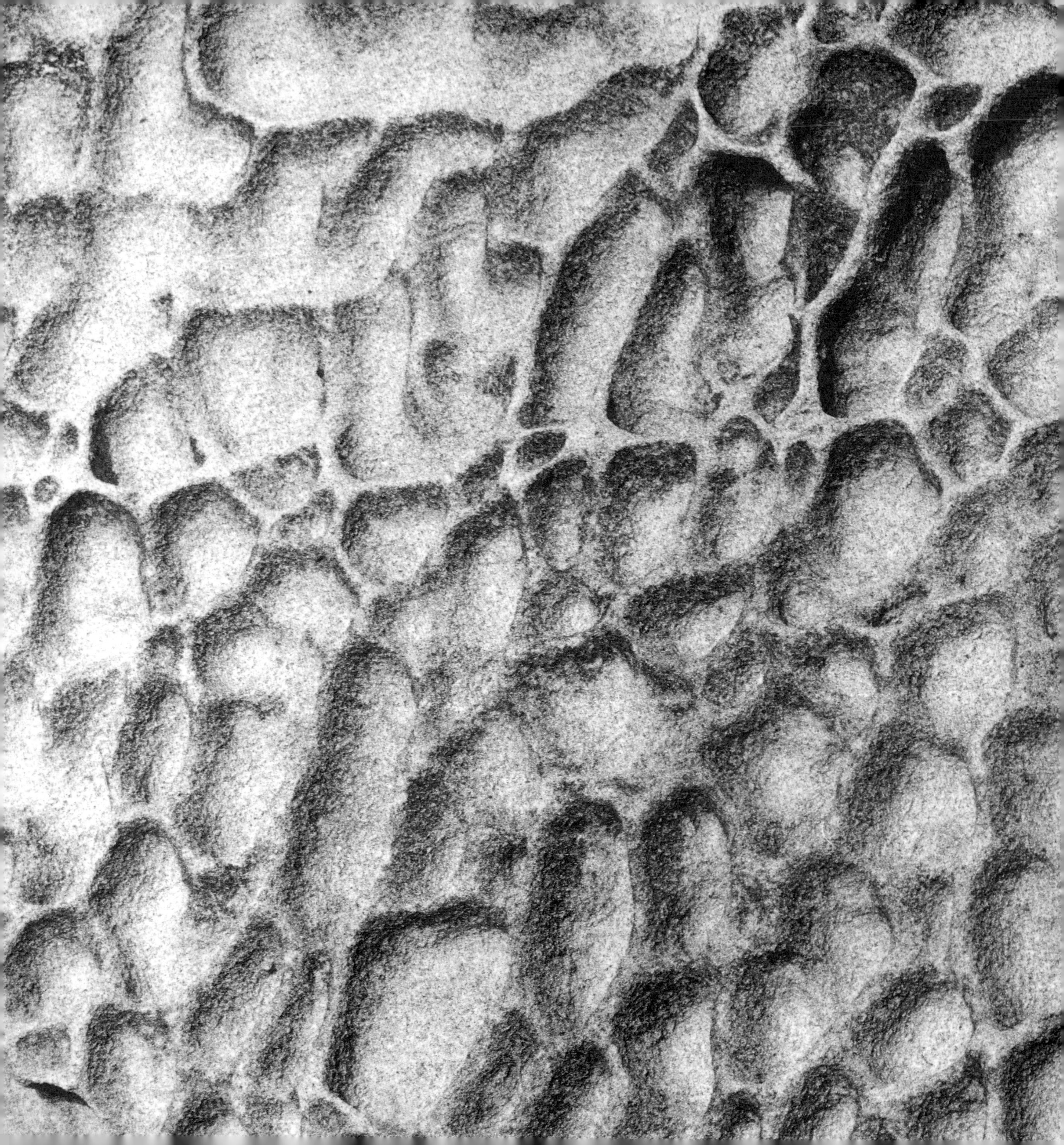